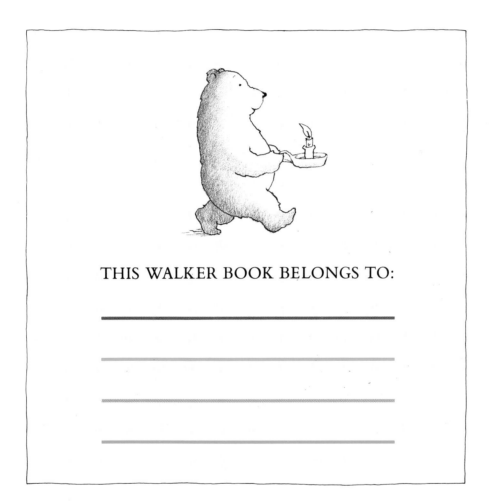

THIS WALKER BOOK BELONGS TO:

For my parents

First published 1984 by Walker Books Ltd
87 Vauxhall Walk, London SE11 5HJ

This edition published 1988
Reprinted 1989, 1990

© 1984 Philippe Dupasquier

Printed and bound in Hong Kong by
Sheck Wah Tong Printing Press Ltd

British Library Cataloguing in Publication Data
Dupasquier, Philippe
The building site. — (Busy places).
I. Title   II. Series
843'.914[J]   PZ7
ISBN 0-7445-0939-4

THE
BUILDING
SITE

PHILIPPE DUPASQUIER

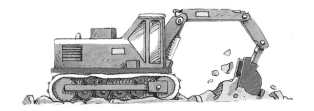

WALKER BOOKS
LONDON

It is early morning.
The building site is quiet.

Nothing disturbs Old Sam or his dog Tinker.

The works van arrives.
'Let's have no dawdling about now, lads,'
says J.K. Biggs, the foreman, to his men.

Aaah! Oooh!
Old Sam and Tinker stretch and yawn.

Scrunch! Scrape! The digger starts to dig.
Rumble! Slurp! The cement truck mixes and pours.
'This way a bit!' Eddie shouts to the crane driver.

'I've told you before to stay off the site,' says J.K. Biggs to Old Sam. 'Just don't come back again, you hear!'

Roar! Clatter! The bulldozer crawls in.
Eddie and Pat direct the crane.

'Just get those bricks laid as quickly as
you can,' says J.K. Biggs to Micky,
the bricklayer, and Ben, his mate.

Thump! Crash! The bulldozer loads
the tip-up truck, while the driver has a chat.

'Hey, Ben, watch that hook!'
Micky calls down, above all the noise.

The surveyor and the architect drive in,
and carefully discuss the plans.

'Help!' yells J.K. Biggs,
suddenly lifted up into the air.

'Bring it straight in!' shouts Jim,
directing the low-loader.

'I've never had such a shock in my life,'
says J.K. Biggs, all white and trembling.

'Straight up! Right a bit! OK!' Jim shouts, as the crane lifts the girders off the low-loader.

Up on the platform everyone stops to watch.
'Not much longer,' thinks J.K. Biggs,
checking the time.

The works van comes to collect the men,
to take them all home.

Two familiar faces watch them go.

The day is over. The site is quiet again.

Old Sam and Tinker make themselves at home.

MORE WALKER PAPERBACKS
For You to Enjoy

BUSY PLACES
by Philippe Dupasquier

The Airport	0-7445-0938-6
The Building Site	0-7445-0939-4
The Factory	0-7445-0978-5
The Garage	0-7445-0937-8
The Harbour	0-7445-0979-3
The Railway Station	0-7445-0977-7

£2.99 each

ROBERT
by Philippe Dupasquier

A small boy with no brothers or sisters but lots of toys, Robert has some very entertaining adventures.

"Popular and comic." *Child Education*

Robert the Great	0-7445-1061-9
Robert the Pilot	0-7445-1341-3
Robert and the Red Balloon	0-7445-1710-9

£2.99 each

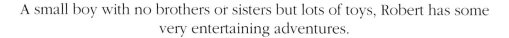